How to Determine Personality

Hiriyappa.B, Ph.D.

Contents

Chapter 1. Personality and Concept of Personality
Chapter 2. Determinants of Personality
Chapter 3. Personality Theories
Chapter 4. Intrapsychic / Psychoanalytic Theory
Chapter 5. Type Theories
Chapter 6. Trait Theories
Chapter 7. Social Learning Theory
Chapter 8. Development of The Personality
Chapter 9. Big Five Model of Personality
Chapter 10. Personality Traits Influencing Organization Behavior

CHAPTER 1

PERSONALITY AND CONCEPT OF PERSONALITY

INTRODUCTION

We can know our personality and its concepts in a better light with an expert's opinion. A common view about the same includes issues like 'personality shaping', 'influencing others' and 'shaping self' for the better. In a society, we see an array of personalities who shape self with theories.

"Personality is result of the battle for control between id, ego & superego."
Sigmund Freud

"She felt that those who prepared for all the emergencies of life beforehand may equip themselves at the expense of joy."
E.M. Forster
"Howards End"

"Personality in terms of self, an organized, permanent subjectively perceived

entity, which is at the very heart of all our experience."
Carl Rogers

"Personality as that which an individual really is, an internal something that guides and directs all human activities."
Gordon Allport

"Life proceeds in terms of a series of psychological crisis, and personality is a function of their outcome."
Erickson

"Personality is the individual's unique way of making sense out of life experiences."
George Kelly

"The structure of personality is composed of three elements the id, ego and super ego."
Sigmund Freud

"Personality is the sum total of ways in which an individual reacts and interacts with others"
Stephen P Robbins

All these expert opinions reveal:

'Personality', 'Concept of Personality', 'Characteristic of Personality', 'The Natureof Personality', 'Assumptions of Personality', 'Determinants of Personality', 'Personality Theories', 'Types of Theories', 'Descriptive Personality Theories', 'Predictive Personality Theories', 'Prominent Personality Theories', 'Intrapsychic/ Psychoanalytic Theory', 'Freud's structure of personality', 'Defense mechanisms', 'Type Theories', Sheldon's Physiognomy Theory, Carl Jung's 'Extrovert and Introvert Theory', 'Trait Theories', Gordon Allport's 'Trait Theory of Personality', 'Social Learning Theory', 'Observational Learning', and Skinner's 'Behaviorist Learning Theory'.

They also unfold ideas like: 'How personality develops', 'Shaping of the Personality', 'Freud's Five Stages of Personality', Erikson's 'Eight Life Stages', Argyris' 'Immaturity to Maturity Stages', 'Big Five Model of Personality', 'The Big Five Personality Factors', 'Personality Structure', 'Personality Traits influencing organization behavior', 'Self- esteem', 'Self-monitoring' and 'Personality characteristics in organizations'.

DEFINING PERSONALITY

You can gauge and understand 'Personality' to a great extent by understanding its origin. The term 'Personality' is derived from the Latin word *'persona'*, which means 'mask'. It refers to an individual's distinct and relatively enduring pattern of thoughts, feelings, needs, motives, values, attitudes and behaviors. It excludes race, gender, and physical attractiveness.

It refers to the sum total of ways in which an individual reacts and interacts with others.

Personality refers to the distinctive and relatively enduring ways of thinking, feeling, and acting for a particular individual.

Personality entails inner psychological characteristics that determine and reflect how a person responds to his or her environment.

The nature of personality reflects individual differences.

Personality unfolds relatively stable and distinctive patterns of behavior that characterize an individual and his or her reactions to the environment. Personality is a relatively stable set of characteristics that influences an individual's behavior.

It is unique and relatively consistent with the pattern of thinking, feeling and behaving.

It refers to preferences for 'situation handling', 'humor sense', or your expectations of others.

All these things vary from one person to the other.

CONCEPT OF PERSONALITY

You can understand the theoretical background of personality and it influence on individuals. 'You are very interesting to know' is a concept of personality with certain individual. When it comes to perception, it varies from one individual to another individual

It refers to personal characteristics that lead to consistent patterns of behavior in an individual.

It is to find the varying behavior in an individual.

It associates with both 'the person' and 'the situation'; it leads to significant behavior markers in organizations.

Consequently, it reinforces the importance of properly managing the situations that comprises employees in a workspace.

It is a complex pattern of deeply embedded psychological characteristics and they are:
- Largely unconscious
- Cannot be eradicated easily

Express them automatically in every facet of functioning.

It involves intrinsic and pervasive factors. These traits emerge from a complicated matrix of biological disposition and experiential learning.

It comprises the individual's distinctive pattern of 'Perceiving', 'Thinking', 'Feeling' and 'Coping'.

CHARACTERISTIC OF PERSONALITY

Do you want to know your personality and its characteristics? You can observe yourself and know the behavior of body and mind and acquire results on the same. The result of an individual is outlined in certain ways:

It is an abstraction, which is based on inferences that is derived from behavioral observation of a person.

Personality differs from person to person. The distinguishing features of personalities facilitate clarity for individuals. It refers to an evolving process that is subject to a variety of internal and external influences, including genetic and biological propensities, social experience and changing environmental circumstances.

THE NATURE OF PERSONALITY

Do you have an interest in knowing the nature of the personality of an individual?

Nature of personality refers to the following issues, which explain an individual's personality:

It develops over a person's lifetime.

Generally, it is stable in the context of work.

It can influence career choices, job satisfaction, stress, leadership, and even performance.

ASSUMPTIONS OF PERSONALITY

You are willing to know assumptions of personality that are associated with individual.

There are three basic assumptions that are listed below:

Personality is relatively stable and therefore predictable in an individual.

Personality is relatively stable across situations of an individual.

People differ in terms of personality traits that they possess; no two people are exact replicas on all traits.

CHAPTER 2

DETERMINANTS OF PERSONALITY

INTRODUCTION

You are willing to find various determinants, which ascertain the actual personality of an individual person. Determinants can be factors that are biological, cultural, family, social and situational in nature and these factors aredirectly or indirectly influenced by an individual's behavior. Personality, as it has been researched, of an individual is different from the other. Therefore, we shall study the major determinants of personality.

DETERMINANTS OF PERSONALITY

You can know the major determinants of personality that ascertain the behavior of an individual and how they act in the society. These determinants are outlined as:

- Biological Factors
- Cultural Factors
- Family Factors
- Social Factors
- Situational Factors

Biological Factors

You observe yourself and find biological factors. Biological factors are hereditary; and then there are Brain, Biofeedback and physical features.

You can understand this one after the other.

Heredity

It refers to 'Physical Stature', 'Facial Attractiveness', 'Sex', 'Temperament', 'Muscle Composition and Reflexes', 'Energy Level', and 'Biological Rhythms'.

These are the characteristics that are considered to be inherent in an individual and they move in the blood/family line from parents and forefathers.

It plays an important part in determining and individual's personality.

Heredity approach argues that the ultimate explanation of an individual's personality is the molecular structures of the genes, which are located in the chromosomes.

Recent research studies show that young children lend strong support to the power of heredity, and findings show that some personality traits may be built into the same genetic code that affect factors like height and hair color.

Brain

Brain is the second biological approach to determine the personality of individual.

It plays an important role in determining the personality of individual.

Electrical Stimulation of the brain (ESB) and 'Split Brain' psychology results indicate that a better understanding of human personality and behavior might stem from a closer study of the brain.

The definite areas of the human brain are associated with 'pain' and 'pleasure'.

Several research studies shows that these things are true!

Biofeedback

It is the third biological approach to determine personality.

Physiologists and psychologists feel that biological functions like brainwave patterns, gastric and hormonal secretions, and fluctuations in blood pressure and skin temperature were beyond conscious control. Recent researches show that these functions can be consciously controlled through biofeedback techniques.

For this purpose, an individual can learn the internal rhythms of a particular body process through electronic signals that are feedback from equipment, which is wired to the body.

In this process, the person can learn to control the body process through questions.

It is one of the interesting topics for futuristic research work in the personality domain.

Physical Features

It is third biological approach to determine personality.

It is a vital ingredient of the personality.

It focuses on an individual person's external

appearance, which also determines the personality.

Physical features like 'tall or short', 'fat or skinny', 'black or white' also come into play. These physical features will influence the personal effect on others and also affect the self-concept of individual.

Recent research studies show that this feature influences an individual's personality in an organization in a definite way.

In totality, heredity would be fixed at birth and no amount of experience can alter them through creation of suitable environment. Apart from this, personality characteristics are not completely dictated by heredity. There are other factors that have an influence when it comes to determining a personality:

Cultural Factors

Each culture expects, and trains its members to behave in ways that are acceptable to the group. To a great degree, the child's cultural group defines the range of experiences and situations he is likely to encounter and the values and personality characteristics that would be reinforced on him.

Paul H Mussen

Cultural factors are also major and they play a vital role in determining an individual's personality.

It refers to traditional practice, customs, procedure, norms and rules and regulation followed by the society.

It significantly influences individual behavior compare to biological factors.

Cultural factors determine attitudes towards independence, aggression, competition, co-operation, positive thinking, team sprit, and also towards a host of human beings. This helps an individual in better discharge of his/her duties towards responsibilities for self and towards society.

Western culture has influenced the Indian society in a big way. Cultural factors also determine the personality.

Family Factors

Family factors are a major influence in determining an individual personality.

A family, at the bare minimum, consists of husband and wife and their children.

A family plays a very important role is nurturing and shaping a personality.

A family plays multiple roles-'guide', 'supervisor', 'care- taker' and 'care-giver'. They influence and trigger co-operation, co-ordination and introduce roles like responsibilities towards family, society and the world.

Family either directly or indirectly influences a person's development of personality.

Social Factors

Social factors are also major chips, which aid and influence the process of determining an individual's personality.

It involves the reorganization of individual's personality in an organization or society.

It refers to acquisition of wide range of personality traits by blending in the society or in a work organization.

The process of socialization starts from home and extending to work environment.

It focuses on good relationships, co-operation, co-ordination and interaction among the members in the society or an organization or a family.

In totality, environmental factors consist of cultural factors, family factors, and social factors.

Situational Factors

Situational factors influence causes that ultimately lead to determining a personality.

Situational factors are very important to change the individual behavior in a different circumstance at different situations. It also influences the personality of an individual person.

In general, personality is stable and consistent, but it does change in different situations.

The interaction of 'Personality' and 'Situational Factors' are outlined this way:
Strong situational pressures
Personality may not predict behavior Example: enforcement of rules Weak Situational pressures Personality may predict behavior Example: Customer sales reps

A strong situation can overwhelm the effects of individual personalities by providing strong cues for appropriate behavior.

CHAPTER 3
PERSONALITY THEORIES

INTRODUCTION
If you are willing to predict the individual behavior, you are likely to learn various personality types and the theories associated with it. Personality type theory aims to classify people into distinct CATEGORIES-- the people belong to descriptive and predictive functions in psychology. In other words, it refers to elaborate speculations or hypothesis about why people behave as they do.

TYPES OF THEORIES
You have to be predictive about which type of personality theory is more meaningful to find comprehensive behavior of an individual. Good personality theory provides a meaningful context within the framework of human behavior and it can be consistently explained and interpreted and the types of theories in personality are outlined below:

Descriptive Theories
Predictive Theories

If you are willing to predict the behavior of an individual, you can gauge various descriptive and predictive theories and its application on individual will help you draw and predict results.

Descriptive Personality Theories

It refers to organize human behavior systematically and it renders it intelligently.

In other words, 'Descriptive theories' provide a meaningful framework for simplifying and integrating all events or set of events.

Descriptive theory provides a meaningful context within the framework of human behavior and it can be consistently explained and interpreted.

Predictive Personality Theories

Predictive personality theory provides a basis for the prediction of events and the outcome, which has yet not transformed into reality.

This theory must be testable and it could be confirmed or dejected in real situations.

PROMINENT PERSONALITY THEORIES

You are without knowing the prominent personality theories. You cannot predict the behavior of an individual and, therefore, you must know the prominent personality theories.

Researchers have developed a number of personality theories and there is no theory that is complete. Therefore, many prominent personalities theories can be conveniently grouped under these five heads:

Intrapsychic Theory
Type Theories Trait
Theories
Social Learning
Theory Self Theory

CHAPTER 4

INTRAPSYCHIC / PSYCHOANALYTIC THEORY

INTRODUCTION

You are now willing to apply Sigmund Freud personality theory on an individual and obtain result. Individual personality is influenced from conscious and unconscious activities of an individual.

Intrapsychic / Psychoanalytic Theory has been developed by Sigmund Freud. This human psychological make up comprises three structural components—'Id', 'Ego' and 'Super Ego'. These three components form every individual's behavior.

FREUD'S STRUCTURE OF PERSONALITY

You are willing to understand yourself in terms of conscious and unconscious activities of your brain, mind and body. Freud's Structure of Personality consists of 'Id', 'Ego' and 'Super Ego'. Freudian Theory is the representation of the interrelationship amid the 'Id', 'Ego', and 'Superego'. The theory determines that 'Conscious' of an individual concerns with the awareness of body and mind and also about the easily known self. The 'Unconscious' of an individual concerns self with matters of low awareness, difficult-to-gauge issues.

Id

It refers to the origin of personality.

It is irrational, impulsive and obedient to the 'pleasure principle'.

It consists of everything psychologically that was inherited and was present at the time of birth.

It refers a storehouse of all instincts, containing dark depths like all wishes, desires, that unconsciously direct and determine human behaviour.

It is oriented towards 'immediate gratification'.

The 'Id' is selfish.

The 'Id' acts without regard to consequence.

It is largely childish, irrational, never satisfied, demanding and destructive for others and self.

'Reflex actions' and 'primary process thinking' are used by 'Id' for obtaining gratification of instinctual urges.

Primary process refers to an attempt to

discharge a tension by forming a mental image of the desired to ease the tension. But this kind of tension release is temporary and mental and it would not satisfy the real need.

Reflex actions refer to the tension release that is reflected in the behavior of individuals like 'blinking of eyes', 'raising eyebrows', 'rubbing the cheeks' etc.

'Id' in totality is instinctive, and it often refers to the 'unconscious', 'unrecognized' and 'unaffected' and it works against socially or culturally determined restrictions and norms.

It basically caters to an individual's natural urges and feelings.

Ego

It refers to a system that mediates between the Id and Superego. The ego tries to balance these two opposing forces according to reality principles.

Ego functions on 'reality principle'.

Serves to balance the demands that are created by 'Id' and the 'Superego'.

Ego assesses what is realistically possible when it comes to satisfying the urges of 'Id' or 'Superego' or both (i.e., what society will deem acceptable)

Ego uses defense mechanisms to protect itself.

Ego is the coherent organization of

mental processes that develops out of Id energy and it has access to consciousness, and it is devoted to reality before giving in to Id's needs and temptations.

It adapt to outside world.

It is said to be the executive part of the personality because it controls the gateway to action, selects the features of the environment to which it will respond and decide which instincts actually need to be satisfied.

It is guided by the Secondary Process (including intellectual operations like thinking, evaluating, planning, and decision-making that determine whether certain behaviors are beneficial)

It is the bridge to reality but not totally conscious.

Ego's reaction to threatening instincts is stress/anxiety.

So, Ego calls upon Defense Mechanisms (internal, unconscious, and automatic psychological strategies for coping and regaining control over id instincts).

Ego performs the following tasks:

It observing accurately what exists in the outside world - 'Perceiving'.

It records these experiences carefully-- 'Remembering'.

Superego

'Superego' is opposite to 'Id' in many ways. It internalise society's rules. It works to prevent the 'Id' from seeking selfish gratification.

Its function is based on 'idealistic principle'.

It refers to our moral guide/conscience.

It is influenced as it has internalized our parents' values and the voice of the society.

It works against the 'Id' by inflicting guilt.

Superego is the representation of society in personality that incorporates norms and standards of culture.

A kid adopts society's rules, regulations, and codes of right and wrong.

'Introjection' is the process where personality incorporates norms and standards of its culture through identification with or without parents or role models of society.

It operates according to 'Morality Principle' (a code concerning society's values)

It refers to conscience (internal agent punishing people when they do wrong; guilt)

It helps in controlling 'Id' impulses by directing energy toward inhibiting Id's expression of sexual and aggressive instincts.

It seeks to suppress needs of Id rather than satisfy them.

It illogically is striving for 100% perfection.

Superego can result in feelings of pride and self-respect through the influence of the Ego (positive standards in form of internal representations of idealized parental figures)

In totality, this theory indicates towards personality and its structure that emerges from the battle for control between 'Id', 'Ego' and 'Superego'. If tension and anxiety grips a person, he resorts to defense mechanisms in order to reduce tensions.

Defensive Mechanisms

These defensive mechanisms are listed below:

Denial

It refers to denying the anxiety outright by the affected person.

Repression

It is blocking out/prevention of anxiety-- forcing anxiety back into unconscious.

Rationalization

It is creating false reasons or explanations for anxiety in the form of a shortcoming.

Projection
It is seeing in others unacceptable feelings that reside in one's own unconscious.

Displacement
It is acting out your anxiety on an innocent party.

Reaction formation
It is reversing the nature of the anxiety.

It is exaggerated love for someone you unconsciously hate.

Sublimation
It is channeling anxiety into socially-acceptable activities

It is focusing sexual energy into art, music, etc.

CHAPTER 5

TYPE THEORIES

INTRODUCTION

It is very difficult to measure an individual's exact personality and behavior. For this, you would have to measure the development of personality and an individual's behavior. You have to apply type theories to obtain the outcome. Type theories represent an attempt to scientifically explain personalities by classifying individual into convenient categories. Some of the examples of Type theories are listed below:

Sheldon's Physiognomy theory
Carl Jung's Extrovert and Introvert theory

Sheldon's Physiognomy Theory

William Sheldon presented this theory.

It is a unique body type temperamental model which represents a link between anatomical / psychological traits and characteristics of an individual with his behavior.

Sheldon has identified some

relationship between the 'physique types' of individuals and their 'personality temperaments'. He has identified three body types:
Endomorph
Mesomorph
Ectomorph

Endomorph

He is bulky and a beloved person.

The person seeks comfort, loves fine food, eats too much, is jovial, affectionate and is liked by all.

Mesomorph

A Mesomorph is basically strong, athletic and tough.

He is fond of muscular activity; he tends to be highly aggressive and self-assertive.

Ectomorph

It refers to people who are thin, long and poorly developed physically.

He leads the league in the intellectual department.

He is labeled as absent-minded and shy but brilliant.

William Sheldon classified personalities according to body type. He called this: 'a

person's *somatotype'*. Sheldon identified three main somatotypes as follows:
- Endomorph [viscerotonic]
- Mesomorph [somatotonic]
- Ectomorph [cerebrotonic]

Endomorph Character and Shape

Endomorph person's character are relaxed, sociable, tolerant, comfort-loving, peaceful and body shape is big, high body fat, often pear shaped, with a high tendency to store body fat.

Mesomorph Character and Shape

Mesomorph person's character are active, assertive, vigorous, combative and body shape is muscular.

Ectomorph Character and Shape

Ectomorph person's character are quiet, fragile, restrained, non-assertive, sensitive and body shape is lean, delicate, poor muscles

One of the potential demerits of this theory is the inherent generalization.

CARL JUNG'S EXTROVERT AND INTROVERT THEORY

Extrovert and Introvert theory proposed and developed by Carl Jung. This theory consists of two parts:

Extroverts
Introverts

Extroverts

An extrovert refers to an optimistic, outgoing, gregarious, and sociable individual. Extroverts are basically objective individuals. They are the 'doers'.

Introverts

Introverts are more inward-directed people. They are less sociable, withdrawn and absorbed in inner life.

They will be guided by their own ideas and philosophy.

They are rigid and less flexible.

In some cases, few people are complete introverts or extroverts, although; however, the mixture of these two ingredients determines the kind of overall personality that an individual would develop.

Jung theory explains the personality and it is based on four dimensions. The four dimensions are:

Thinking - It refers to logical reasoning

Feeling - The interpretation of a thing or an event on a subjective scale

Sensation - It deals with the perception of a thing in its general sense.

Intuition - It is based on the unconscious inner perception of the potentialities or events or things.

CHAPTER 6

TRAIT THEORIES

INTRODUCTION

Since traits are ever changing from one individual to another, it is difficult to predict the exact trait that defines an individual unless you are interested in knowing trait theories and its application on individuals and the result variance.

A 'Personality' consists of broad dispositions, which are called traits. Traits tend to lead to characteristic responses. People can be described in terms of basic ways in which they behave; are they outgoing and friendly or are they dominant and assertive?

BASIC FIVE FACTORS

You want to know basic five factors that are applied to measure the personality and behavior of the individual. Five factors influence an individual's personality and behavior. These factors are unfolded below:

Emotional stability

It is about being calm rather than

anxious, secure rather than insecure, and self-satisfied than self-pitying.

Extraversion

It is about being sociable instead of retiring, fun-loving instead of sober, and affectionate instead of being reserved.

Openness

It is about being imaginative rather than practical, preferring variety to routine, and being independent rather than conforming.

Agreeableness

It is about being softhearted and not ruthless, trusting and not suspicious, and helpful instead of being non co-operative.

Conscientiousness

It is about being organized rather than disorganized, careful rather than careless, and discipline over impulsiveness.

Individualism— It is about giving priority to personal goals rather than group goals; it emphasizes values that serve the self such as feeling good, personal distinction, and independence.

Collectivism — It emphasizes values that serve the group by subordinating personal goals to preserve group integrity.

A personality trait can be defined as 'an enduring attribute of a person that appears constantly in a variety of situations'.

FUNDAMENTAL ASSUMPTIONS OF TRAIT THEORIES

You have to know basic assumptions of trait theories. Certain fundamental assumptions of trait theories are listed below:

Traits distinguish one personality from the other.

Individuals can be described in terms of construction of traits like 'affiliation', 'achievement', 'anxiety', 'aggression' and 'dependency'.

Traits can be quantified and they do not defy measurements.

Traits that a person has is assumed to be fairly stable, and the difference in personality and behavior between two individuals is assumed to be the result of differences in the amount of traits that each person has.

Type theory is an extension of type theory. There are two most commonly known trait theories that are listed below:

Gordon Allport's
Raymond Cattle's

GORDON ALLPORT'S TRAIT THEORY OF PERSONALITY

Gordon Allport defined personality as "the dynamic organization of those internal psychophysical systems that determine a person's characteristic behavior and thought. Within the individual, personality is real. It is "what a person really is". It relatively is enduring, consistent and inferred from the behavior.

There are three types of traits as listed below:

Cardinal traits

It affects every area of the individual's life.

It refers to Mother Theresa – altruistic.

Central traits

It influences many aspects of our lives, but not quite as pervasive.

It refers to someone you think of as "kind" or "funny".

Secondary traits

It affects narrower aspects of our lives.

It refers to preference for cowboy hats or to wear a perfume at all times.

Allport's Trait theory reflects the following things:

A strong commitment to the assumptions of rationality, proactive behavior, and heterostasis.

A moderate commitment to the holism and the ability to assume.

A moderate commitment to the assumption of freedom and subjectivity

A midrange position on 'Constitutionalism'—'Environmentalism' and '**Changeability**'— and exchangeability dimensions.

It is about studying of values and it is a self-report for personality test. In totally, a personality can be characterized by its dominant value orientation or by their particular patterns of a person's value system.

CHAPTER 7

SOCIAL LEARNING THEORY

INTRODUCTION

An individual's personality is developed through self-experience, experience with others and through an environment that is the result of personality molding. Albert Bandura's social learning theory depicts psychological functioning in terms of the continuous reciprocal interaction of behavior, and cognitive and environmental influences. Social Learning emphasizes on the peculiar power of learning through 'social rewards' and 'punishments', including vicarious reinforcements and modeling.

Social Learning Theory includes study of the following issues:
Motivation
Emotion
Cognition Social-reinforcement
Reinforcing Self
Vicarious emotional arousal
Vicarious reinforcement
Semantic generalization
Rule-based learning
Efficient learning method includes

following issues:
- Attention
- Retention
- Production
- Performance (Motivation)

The social learning theory is based on:

Personality development is largely a result of social variables than biological drives.

Motives can be traced to know conscious needs and wants rather than unconscious and latent desires.

OBSERVATIONAL LEARNING

This is a key concept in social learning theory. It involves the following issues for observational learning:

It is more prevalent and efficient than classical or operant learning.

Mostly, it is human behavior and attitude learned through observation intentionally or acquired accidentally.

It begins at a very early age

Example: It is the basis of, to a great extent, early language acquisition.

It can exceed imitation: The observer can learn from the model's mistakes as well as success.

It can result in synthesis of different behaviors, which then leads to innovative and creative behaviors.

It can acquire internal standards for evaluating self and other's behavior.

This behavior is maintained by expectancies or anticipated consequences

Behavior is learned and ultimately repeated due to 'attention', 'retention', 'production' and 'motivation'.

Attention

It refers to undivided focus: similarity; status; competence; power; attraction. Simpler behaviors are more readily imitated; young children readily copy aggressive behaviors.

Retention

It refers to use of 'imagery', 'language' and 'encoding of rehearsal'.

Production

It refers to a capacity to produce response.

Motivation

It refers to the observer, motivated to perform the behavior in terms of reinforcement, and punishment and reward systems.

Social learning theory started in an attempt to retain behaviorism's empirical rigor and some of its basic principles at the same time as trying to expand beyond: What behaviorism can be explained and predicted? There are three important aspects related to behaviorism. They are 'motivation', 'emotion' and 'cognition'.

Furthermore, it came to be realized that so many of the things that reinforce our behavior are not related to physical needs but to psychological needs. Social Reinforcements like 'acceptance', 'hugs', 'approval', 'interest', 'praise', and 'attention' among others are extremely important in making people continue to perform in a particular way behaviorally. In this sense, the learning theory becomes socially oriented.

Social learning theory claims that people 'think', 'plan', 'perceive' and 'believe'. It is an important part of learning.

SKINNER'S BEHAVIORISTIC LEARNING THEORY OF PERSONALITY

It is characterized by the rejection of an inner 'autonomous man' as the cause of human actions and a disregard for physiological genetic explanations of behavior.

Skinner claims that behavior is lawful determined, predictable, and environmentally controlled.

Skinner's basic assumptions about

human nature are strong and explicit. Behaviouristic learning theory reflects a strong commitment to 'Determinism', 'Elementalism', 'Environmentalism', 'Changeability', 'Objectivity', 'Reactivity' and 'Knowability'.

The basic assumptions of rationality, irrationality and homeostasis are not applicable to Skinner's position since he rejects internal sources of behavior.

CHAPTER 8

DEVELOPMENT OF THE PERSONALITY

INTRODUCTION

If you are inclined to develop your personality, you are bound to learn the various stages of life, which an individual goes through.

A 'Personality' can develop with advancement in an individual's age as he passes through certain stages in a sequentialorder of life. Different psychologists and behavioral scientists have come up with different stages, which explain how an individual's personality develops or shapes. Important researches are underpinned for discussion: How personality develops and how the shaping of an individual's personality occurs?

   Freud's Five Stages of Personality
   Erikson's Eight Life Stages
   Argyris' Immaturity to Maturity Stages

FREUD'S FIVE STAGES OF PERSONALITY

Freud's personality stages are based on the belief that events that once occurred in an individual's childhood have their bearing on adulthood and in turn, create and shape behavior in adulthood. According to Freud, there are five stages of psychological development that shape an individual's personality.

FREUD'S FIVE STAGES OF PERSONALITY

You can know of Freud's five stages of personality:

   The Oral stage
   The Anal Stage
   The Phallic Stage
   The Latency Stage
   The Genital Stage

The Oral Stage

Oral Stage refers to time frame of birth to one year of a child.

It focuses upon satisfying needs of mouth and digestive tract including tongue and lips.

It is aim of Eros. Self-preservation is made possible by nourishment through mouth.

Major characteristics are interest in oral gratification from thumb sucking, eating, mouthing and biting.

Oral receptive personality type is derived from childhood pleasures of receiving food and digesting it. Relationships depend upon others. Gullible personalities are interested in getting info and knowledge on material goods and they 'will swallow anything'.

Oral aggressive personality type is derived from childhood pleasures of 'mouth', 'food', and 'eating', but with or without 'chewing', 'biting', or 'use of teeth'. They seek to hold others firmly. They are aggressive in relationships with others.

The Anal Stage

Anal Stage refers to second and third year of a child.

It involves sexual gratification that leads to relief in the 'bowel' and in stimulated 'anus'.

It involves toilet training (issue of interpersonal interaction and conflict between parent and child).

Anal Retention is delay of final satisfaction until the last possible moment. Always 'save' for the future.

Anal Expulsive is inclination to disregard for accepted rules of cleanliness, orderliness, and appropriate behavior. React against others' attempts to restrict them by doing what they want whenever and wherever. Messiness, sloppiness, aggressive destructiveness, tempers tantrums, emotional outbursts and cruelty form a part of it.

Major characteristics are gratification from expelling and withholding feces and toilet training.

The Phallic Stage

Phallic Stage refers to fourth and fifth years for a child.

It involves satisfaction through masturbation.

It is the last infantile stage.

It provides context where two important complexes develop and critical issues of anxiety and envy become relevant.

It is the basis of psychological and social identification for children.

It involves results in psychological and sex-role differences.

It determines development of superego.

This stage creates difference between boys and girls.

In this stage, boys have possessive love for mothers and see fathers as rivals (this thinking is influenced by Greek myth of Oedipus).

Oedipus complex is feelings, desires, and strivings revolving around a boy's desire for mother and consequent hatred towards father.

Electra complex is love of dad for daughters and hatred for mothers.

Final step of Oedipal complex is formation of superego.

Fixated male may devote life to sexual promiscuity in quest for sexual gratification.

Freud believes that female superego develops less holistically than males.

The Latency Stage

Latency Stage refers to six and twelve of a child.

This stage is notable for absence of dominant erogenous zone.

In this stage, children lay aside attraction to parents and become sexually disinterested.

In this stage, libidinous instincts are transformed through sublimation. (Sublimation: It is a process reorienting instinctual aims that are more personally and culturally acceptable.)

A teen fixed in anal stage might be interested in clay substituting earlier desires to play with feces.

The Genital Stage
Genital Stage refers to (puberty +)

This stage includes mature sexual love; directing feelings of lust and affection towards others.

First 3 stages revolve around 'Cathexes' (attachments of libidinal energy to external world objects or fantasizing internal images). Pre-genital stage cathexis is typified by self-centered images. Genital stage cathexis is directed less towards bodily pleasure but more towards emotional pleasure.

In this stage, one tends to seek sexual gratification through heterosexual love and attraction.

One takes interest in opposite sex.

ERIKSON'S EIGHT LIFE STAGES

Erikson has depicted development of personality into eight stages that are more systematic in manner, and he has identified with eight stages of human life. Erikson has asserted that each stage is overwhelmed by conflicts, which need to be resolved successfully before an individual moves to the next stage. Movement from one stage to next stage requires development. At this time, movement can even involve regression i.e., from next stage to earlier stage when events are of a traumatic nature.

Eight Life Stages are listed below:

Infancy
Early Childhood
Play Age
School Age
Adolescence
Young Adulthood
Adulthood
Old Age (Sunset Age)

Infancy

It refers to first year of life of a child and it is characterized by trust or mistrust.

The infants raised in loving and affectionate atmosphere learn to trust others.

Lack of love and affection leads to mistrust for a person.

This bears long lasting impact on one's personality and in the resultant behavior.

Early Childhood

This stage spreads between the age of two and three years of a child.

In this stage, the child starts to acquire independence.

In this period, when the child is allowed to do it he feels autonomy. If disallowed, it can create a sense of shame and it may develop doubt in a child.

Play Age

It is the age between four and five years of a child.

In this stage, the child seeks to discover what can be done.

In this case, the child is allowed and encouraged to do what he wants to do; the child develops a sense of initiative. In spite of this, if the child is discouraged to do, he feels lack of self-confidence.

School Age

It refers to child's age in school from six to twelve years of age.

It is useful for child to learn knowledge and skills.

In this stage, if child makes progress compatible with his abilities, it develops a sense of industry in the child.

Its opposite results in a sense of inferiority.

Adolescence

It refers to children during their teenage period when they try to gain a sense of identity for themselves in the society.

In this case, they do not want to become confused about who they are.

In this stage, a person wants autonomy, initiative and industry developed in earlier stages. It helps teenagers in gaining identity for themselves.

Young Adulthood

It refers to the young in his twenties. He tries to develop deep and permanent relationship with others to have a feeling of intimacy.

Failing in it results in a sense of isolation.

Adulthood

It refers to the adults in the age group of forties and fifties. They face the situation to procreate or self-absorption.

Adults, who are productive in terms of work, raise children with serious concern and guide the next generation. They are called generative.

Self-absorbed adults do not look beyond themselves in this stage.

During this stage, they are absorbed in their career development and maintenance.

Old Age (Sunset Age)

It refers to old age of the person. It is the adulthood that allows a sense of wisdom.

In old age, he/she appreciates continuity of past, present and future, and he become fully satisfied.

In this stage, fear of death is dispelled.

In this stage, the reverse situation results in a sense of despise, fear from death, desire, desire for living a second time and depression.

ARGYRIS IMMATURITY TO MATURITY STAGES

Harvard Professor Chris Argyris identified distinct stages in one's personality development. He has postulated that all healthy people seek like situations, which can offer them autonomy, equality, and the opportunity to show their ability and competence with complexity.

According to him, the healthy people follow seven dimensions to move from immaturity to maturity:

From passivity to activity

From dependence to independence

From selective behavior to diverse behavior

From shallow interest to deep interest

From short-time perspective to long-time perspective

From subordinate position to superordinate position

From lack of self-awareness to self

awareness and control

CHAPTER 9
BIG FIVE MODEL OF PERSONALITY

INTRODUCTION

The Big Five model shapes personality and behavior of an individual. It influences your job behavior and performance.

BIG FIVE MODEL OF PERSONALITY

Big five model of personality influences the job behavior and job performances. It is popularly known as the 'Big Five Model of Personality'. These vital traits about this model are listed below:

Extraversion
Neuroticism
Agreeableness
Openness to Experience
Conscientiousness

Extraversion (Positive Affectivity)
It refers to positive affectivity factors

of the Big Five Model of personality.

It includes a personality trait that predisposes individuals to experience positive emotional states, feel good about themselves and the world around them.

Extraversion is classified as extraverts and introversion is classified as introverts for positive affectivity in an organization.

It indicates the relationship with others in an organization.

It principally consists of sociability, talkativeness and assertiveness; these are used for improvement of employee performance and their behavior in an organization.

Neuroticism (Negative Affectivity)

It refers to negative affectivity factors of the Big Five Model of personality.

It refers to a personality trait that reflects people's tendency to experience negative emotional states, feeling of distress, and general views about themselves and the world around them in a negative light.

In this case, employee performance is reduced and leads to high absence in workspace.

Agreeableness

It refers to agreeable people. They are co-operative, warm and trusting with their behavior.

This type of trait is very important to business and for its clients to achieve their goals and objectives.

It is about the personality trait that captures the distinction between individuals who get along well in comparison to people who do not.

Agreeable people traits are always high and non-agreeable people traits are low.

Conscientiousness

It is one of the important factors of the Big Five model.

It refers to the personality trait that describes the extent to which an individual is careful, scrupulous, and persevering.

It measures reliability in terms of behavior that is organized, dependable and consistent with job performance.

Openness to Experience

It refers to the personality trait that captures the extent to which an individual is

Original

Open to a wide variety of

stimuli Has broad interests

And is willing to take risks as opposed to being narrow-minded and cautious

THE BIG FIVE PERSONALITY FACTORS

Personality structure refers to the big five personality factors. Each factor is a continuum of many related traits in this personality structure. The Big Five Personality factors are outlined below:

Extroversion

Agreeableness

Conscientiousness

Emotional Stability

Openness To Experience

PERSONALITY STRUCTURE

Personality structure refers to different traits, which a person depicts in different circumstances. They are as below:

Adjustment

A person depicts adjustment structure who is stable, confident, effective, nervous, self-doubting.

Sociability

A person depicts adjustment structure who is gregarious, energetic, self-dramatizing, shy and unassertive.

Conscientiousness

A person depicts adjustment structure who is planful, neat and dependable, impulsive, and careless.

Agreeableness

A person depicts adjustment structure who is warm, tactful, considerate and independent.

Intellectual Openness
A person depicts adjustment structure who is imaginative, curious, original, dull, unimaginative.

CHAPTER 10

PERSONALITY TRAITS INFLUENCING ORGANIZATION BEHAVIOR

INTRODUCTION

Some of the most important personality attributes will determine how one will behave in an organization. It can be explained below:

LOCUS OF CONTROL

Locus of control refers to one's belief that what happens is either within one's control (that is internal) or beyond one's control (that is external). Locus of control factors are internal factors and external factors. Internal factors are controllable factors of one's belief and External factors are uncontrollable factors of one's beliefs and circumstances.

Those who have internal locus of control, believe that they are the masters of their own fate and ready to control themselves.

Those who have external locus of control, they see themselves as pawns of fate and believe that what happens to them in their lives is due to luck or factors which are beyond their control.

MACHIAVELLIANISM

Machiavellianism refers to Niccolo Machiavelli. He founded Machiavellianism in Sixteenth century.

It refers to the degree to which an individual is pragmatic, maintains emotional distance, and believes that ends can justify means.

Conditions favoring Machiavellianism are outlined below:
- Direct interaction
- Minimal rules and regulations
- Emotions distract for others

SELF ESTEEM

In psychology, self-esteem or self-worth is a person's self-image at an emotional level; circumventing reason and logic. The term differs from ego in that the ego is a more artificial aspect; one can remain highly egotistical, while underneath they have very low self-esteem.

Personality trait that describes the extent to which people have pride in themselves and their capabilities.

Definition of Self-Esteem Self-esteem is "how much a person likes, accepts, and respects himself overall as a person".

CHARACTERISTICS OF LOW SELF-ESTEEM

A teenager with low self-esteem will: Demean his own talents
Feel that others don't value him Feel powerless
Be easily influenced by others Express a narrow range of emotions Avoid situations that provoke anxiety Become defensive and easily frustrated Blame others for their own weaknesses

Low self-esteem has been co-related with low life satisfaction, loneliness, anxiety, resentment, irritability and depression.

CHARACTERISTICS OF HIGH SELF-ESTEEM

A teenager with high self-esteem will: Act independently
Assume responsibility
Be proud of accomplishments
Approach new challenges with enthusiasm
Exhibit a broad range of emotions Tolerate frustration well
Feel capable of influencing others

High self-esteem has been co-related with academic success in high school, internal locus of control, high family outcome, and positive sense of self-attractiveness.

SELF-MONITORING

It refers to the extent to which people try to control the way they present themselves to others.

A personality trait that measures an individual's ability to adjust his or her behavior to external and situational factors.

It refers and related to the adjustment factor of the Big Five model.

If you self-monitor, performance in job will be high and without self-monitoring, in this case, job performance will be low and low job satisfaction would surface.

Self - Monitoring

Behavior based on cues from

people and situations: they are two type of situations.

High self-monitors a Low self-monitors

High self-monitors

High self-monitors are flexible and adjust behavior according to the situation and the behavior of the others. It can be appearing unpredictable and inconsistent.

Low self-monitors

Low self-monitors are act from internal states rather than from situational cues, show consistency and less likely to respond to work group norms or supervisory feedback.

RISK TAKING

Risk taking is different from one-person tasks to other-person tasks.

Avoiding risks or propensity to assume affects a manger's behavior in making decisions.

Research studies show that mangers that will take high risk and make more rapid decisions are required in an organization. A workplace doesn't develop liking for low risk takers as managers.

In general scenario, the propensity to assume risks varies which depends upon the nature of the job.

Type A versus Type B Personality
Type A individuals have an intense desire to achieve; they are extremely competitive; they have a sense of urgency; they are impatient, and can be hostile.

Type B individuals are more relaxed and easy going.

McCLELLAND'S LEARNED NEEDS
McClelland's Learned Needs have traits such as 'need for power', 'need for achievement' and 'need for affiliation' and they also influence an organization. For this purpose, managers should have a high need for achievement and power.

Extroverts and Introverts
An extrovert refers to optimistic, outgoing, gregarious, and sociable individual. Extroverts are basically objective, oriented individuals who are doers.

Introverts refer to more inward directed people.

They are less sociable, withdrawn and absorbed in inner life.

They will be guided by their own ideas and philosophy.

They are rigid and less flexible and

subjectivity oriented.

Authoritarianism

It refers to authoritarian role in an organization.

It finds the negative philosophy of people in an organization.

It discourages group and team work

It centralizes all tasks related to authority in a work organization.

In this way, an individual will get high position of authority in an organization.

PERSONALITY CHARACTERISTICS IN ORGANIZATIONS

Self-Efficacy

Self-Efficacy refers to belief and expectations about one's ability to accomplish a specific task effectively.

Sources of self-efficacy are stated below:

Prior experiences

Behavior models (observing success) Persuasion

Assessment of current physical & emotional capabilities

Self Esteem

In psychology, self-esteem or self-worth is a person's self-image at an emotional level, circumventing reason and logic. The term differs from ego in that 'ego' is a more artificial aspect; one can remain highly egotistical while underneath they might be suffering from low self-esteem.

It is the personality trait that describes the extent to which people have pride in them and in their capabilities.

Self-Monitoring

It refers to the extent to which people try to control the way they present themselves to others.

A personality trait that measures an individual's ability to adjust his or her behavior to external situations

It refers and relates to the adjustment factor of the Big Five model.

If you self- monitor, job performance will be high and without self-monitoring, in this case, job performance is low and low job satisfaction will stem from work.

www.ingramcontent.com/pod-product-compliance
Lightning Source LLC
Chambersburg PA
CBHW030500220526
45464CB00006B/2592